Calendars of Native Americans

Timekeeping Methods of Ancient North America

Lynn George

Math
for the
REAL World™

Rosen Classroom Books & Materials
New York

Published in 2004 by The Rosen Publishing Group, Inc.
29 East 21st Street, New York, NY 10010

Book Design: Haley Wilson

Photo Credits: Cover, p. 24 © Corbis; cover (inset), pp. 14, 16–17 courtesy Museum of the South Dakota
State Historical Society; p. 4 © Bettmann/Corbis; p. 8 © Hulton-Deutsch Collection/Corbis; p. 10 © Richard
Collier, Wyoming State Parks and Cultural Resources Department; p. 12 © Nebraska State Historical Society
Photograph Collections; pp. 20–21 © Artephot/Corbis Sygma; pp. 22–23 © Bill Ross/Corbis; p. 26 © Gianni
Dagli Orti/Corbis; pp. 28, 30 © The Carnegie Museum.

Library of Congress Cataloging-in-Publication Data

George, Lynn
        Calendars of Native Americans : timekeeping methods of
ancient North America / Lynn George.
                p. cm. — (PowerMath)
        Includes index.
        Summary: This book discusses the design and construction
of the Mayan, Aztec, and Native American calendars.
  ISBN 0-8239-8994-1 (lib.)
  ISBN 0-8239-8918-6 (pbk.)
  6 pack ISBN 0-8239-7446-4
        1. Indian calendar—North America—Juvenile literature
[1. Indian calendar—North America]   I. Title   II. Series
        E98.C14 G46 2004   2002-154573
        529'.3297—dc21

Manufactured in the United States of America

Contents

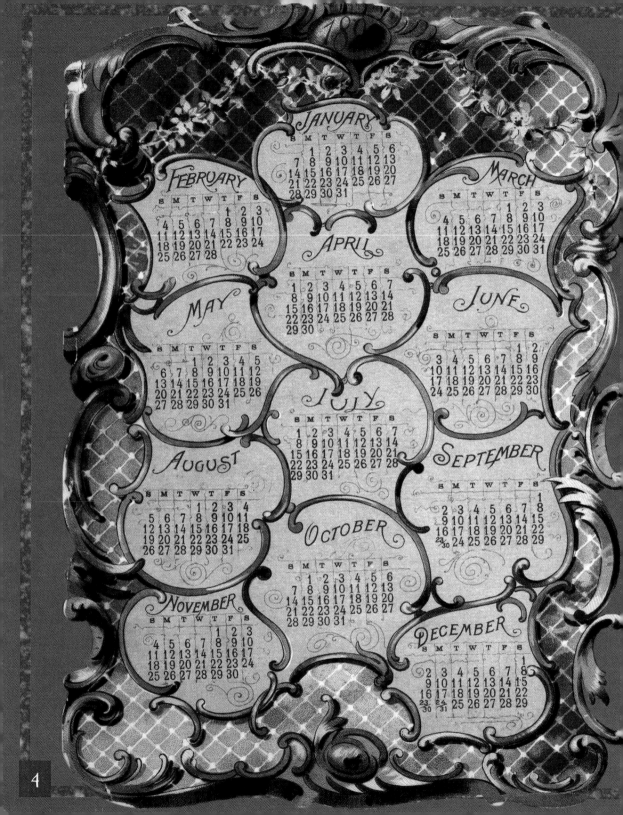

4

Our Calendar

Calendars show how we measure a year. A year is equal to 12 months, or 52 weeks, or 365 days. Each year starts on January 1 and ends on December 31. Calendars show how many days are in each month. January, March, May, July, August, October, and December each have 31 days. April, June, September, and November each have 30 days. February usually has 28 days. Calendars also show the names of the 7 days of the week: Sunday, Monday, Tuesday, Wednesday, Thursday, Friday, and Saturday.

Calendars help us organize our time. They show us what the date will be for Thanksgiving in a certain year, or which day of the week New Year's Day and the Fourth of July will fall on. We use calendars to mark important personal events, such as when we have our big math test or when a school holiday starts.

Some countries have special religious calendars in addition to the kind of calendar shown here. There are about 40 different calendars being used in the world today!

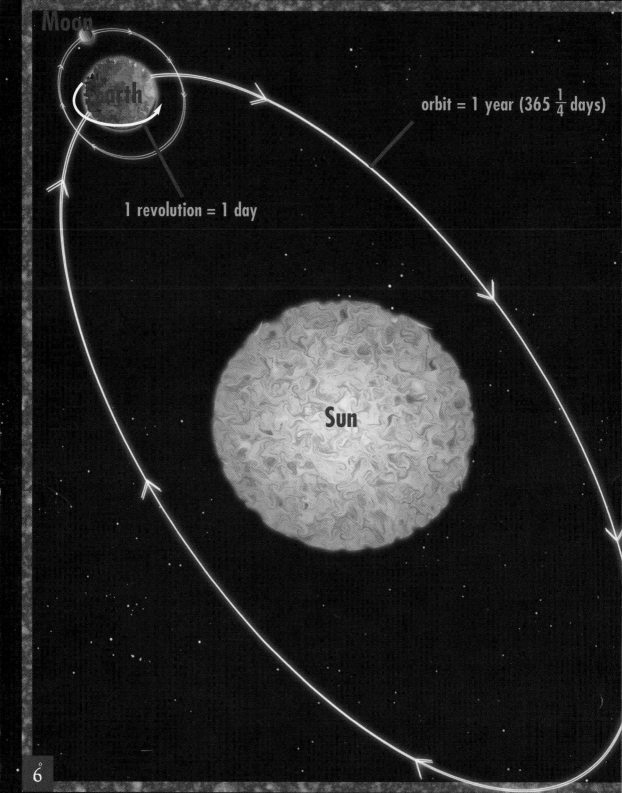

Moon

Earth

orbit = 1 year (365 $\frac{1}{4}$ days)

1 revolution = 1 day

Sun

Our calendar is a solar calendar, which means we measure time by the Sun. Our year is equal to the time it takes for Earth to orbit the Sun once. A day is the time it takes Earth to complete one full turn on its **axis**. We measure this from midnight one day to midnight the next day.

We say that our year has 365 days, but that is not an exact measurement. Earth actually takes $365 \frac{1}{4}$ days to orbit the Sun. This means that our calendar is off by $\frac{1}{4}$ day each year. After 4 years, our calendar is off by a full day: $\frac{1}{4} + \frac{1}{4} + \frac{1}{4} + \frac{1}{4} = 1$. To correct this error, we add an extra day to February once every 4 years. We call that year a "leap year."

The Moon also helped shape our calendar. Our word "month" comes from an old word for "moon." In ancient times, a month was the time from one **new moon** to the next, or the time it took the Moon to orbit Earth. Today, we measure time by the Sun rather than the Moon, so our month is a little longer than an ancient month.

In ancient times, people measured a day from noon one day until noon the next day. That's because noon was the easiest time of day to mark, since the Sun is directly above us at noon.

Medicine Wheel Calendars

Imagine that you were an ancient Native American who did not have the calendar we use today. How would you measure time? Ancient Native Americans actually had their own ways to use the Sun and Moon to measure time. They also watched the movements of the stars to measure time.

The time from one new moon to the next was a month. Changes in the positions of the stars and the Sun throughout the year told ancient Native Americans when to plant crops or hold religious **ceremonies**. These changes also told Native Americans when wild fruits and vegetables would be ripe, and when wild animals would return to the hunting grounds. The Sun was so important to Native Americans from the **Great Plains** of North America that they even painted pictures of it on their clothing. To measure the Sun's position exactly, they built medicine wheels.

Around 1835, an artist named George Catlin painted this picture of a Plains Indian wearing a buffalo skin robe decorated with a picture of the Sun.

Aldebaran

Sunrise on First Day of Summer

Rigel

Sirius

A medicine wheel is a large circle of stones. Rows of stones inside the circle lead from the rim to the center, much like the spokes of a wagon wheel. At the center of the circle is a pile of stones.

There are about 100 medicine wheels on the Great Plains of North America. One of the oldest is the Moose Mountain Medicine Wheel in Canada. It is about 2,000 years old. Others may be even older!

One of the most famous medicine wheels is the Bighorn Medicine Wheel in northern Wyoming. This medicine wheel was probably built about 300 years ago. It is almost 100 feet wide and has 6 small piles of stones around the rim. One of the small piles lines up with one of the spokes to point to the spot on the horizon where the Sun rises on the first day of summer. This helped the Native Americans of the Great Plains know when it was time to plant crops and to hold important religious ceremonies.

The Bighorn Medicine Wheel has three piles of rocks that line up with spokes to point to the positions of the three brightest stars: Aldebaran, Rigel, and Sirius.

Winter Counts

The **Sioux** and other Native Americans of the Great Plains created a different kind of calendar to keep track of the years. They called this calendar the "winter count," since they measured years by winters.

Each year, the tribe's Keeper of the Winter Count chose a single special event to represent the year and added it to his record, which he kept on a buffalo hide. Native Americans did not have a system of writing, so the Keeper drew simple pictures, or **pictographs**, to represent the events. For example, the Keeper might draw an elk with an arrow in it to represent a year in which a great hunt occurred, or a figure of a person to represent the year a great leader died.

The members of a tribe could use the winter count to figure out how many years had passed between certain events, or to figure out how old they were.

This photograph was taken in 1926. It shows Sam Kills Two, a member of the Sioux tribe, adding another pictograph to his winter count.

A winter count was also a record of a tribe's history. The Keeper was responsible for remembering what all the pictures meant, so that he could tell others in the tribe about the tribe's history. The Keeper recorded events such as great hunts, severe storms, battles, heroic deeds, and illnesses that killed many people. Copies of the winter counts were made for related tribes so that everyone would know the tribe's history.

The winter count shown here was made by a man named Lone Dog, who was a member of the Sioux tribe. The events shown on Lone Dog's count start in 1800 and go to 1871. Instead of arranging his count in rows, like some Keepers did, Lone Dog arranged his in a **spiral**. The earliest event is in the center, and the last event is at the end of the outer circle.

Lone Dog's original winter count was made on cowhide. The count was later destroyed by fire. This is one of three copies of it that still exist.

Here are some of the pictographs from Lone Dog's winter count, along with their meanings. Lone Dog did not choose what events he would show by himself. He talked to other tribal leaders, and they made the choices together.

1807–1808
Chief Red-Coat was killed.

1833–1834
A great meteor shower occurred.

1800–1801
The black lines stand for Sioux who were killed by Crow Indians.

1825–1826
Many Native Americans drowned when the Missouri River flooded.

The pictographs don't tell the full stories of the events they represent. They were just signs to remind the Keeper of the stories, so that he could tell the stories to others in the tribe.

1841–1842
Feather-in-the-Ear stole 30 spotted horses.

1865–1866
Many horses died because there was not enough grass for them to eat.

1837–1838
One hundred k were killed on a big hunt.

1853–1854
White men brought striped blankets to Native Americans.

Mayan Calendars

Long before the Native Americans built medicine wheels or made winter counts, the ancient **Maya** created their own calendars. Maya civilization is almost 3,000 years old. The area occupied by the ancient Maya included the part of North America that is now Mexico. The ancient Maya invented three separate calendars, which they used together. Each calendar measured something different.

One calendar was called the long count. The Maya used the long count to count all the days since the world began. According to ancient Mayan beliefs, the world began in 3114 B.C. The ancient Maya believed the long count would end in 2012 A.D.

The ancient Maya also had a calendar with 260 days, which is often called the sacred calendar. Each day in this calendar had a number and a name. The numbers started with 1 and went through 13, then started over again. The names were taken in order from a list of 20 names. After they reached the end of the list of names, they started over with the first one.

The table on page 19 shows how the Maya's system of naming the days of the sacred calendar worked. It also shows meanings for the Mayan words used in the names of the days.

DAY		
Number	Name	English Meaning
1	Imix	Waterlily
2	Ik	Wind
3	Akbal	Night
4	Kan	Corn
5	Chikchan	Snake
6	Kimi	Death's Head
7	Manik	Hand
8	Lamat	Venus
9	Muluk	Water
10	Ok	Dog
11	Chuen	Frog
12	Eb	Skull
13	Ben	Corn Stalk
1	Ix	Jaguar
2	Men	Eagle
3	Kib	Shell
4	Kaban	Earth
5	Etznab	Flint
6	Kawak	Storm Cloud
7	Ahau	Lord
8	Imix	Waterlily
9	Ik	Wind
10	Akbal	Night
11	Kan	Corn
12	Chikchan	Snake
13	Kimi	Death's Head

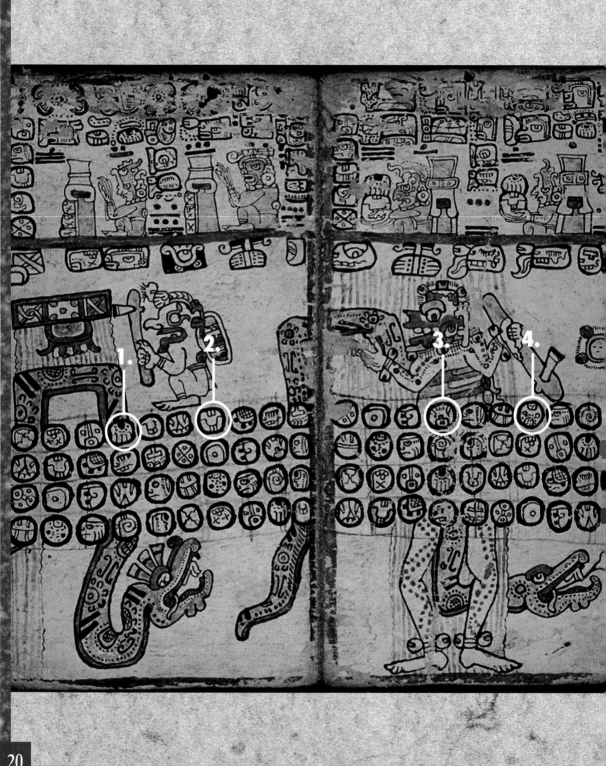

The Maya could not have made their calendars without a great knowledge of **astronomy**. They are still famous today for this knowledge. Their careful study of the movements of the Sun, Moon, and stars helped them to measure time more exactly than anyone else in the ancient world.

The Maya made a record of their knowledge in books like the one shown here. Four rows of circles with drawings inside them stretch across the lower part of the pages. These are the day signs for the days of the sacred calendar.

 1. Imix = Waterlily   2. Kan = Corn

 3. Chuen = Frog   4. Men = Eagle

This almanac was made in the 1200s. It is a manuscript, which means it was written by hand. Some of the day signs from the almanac are shown here, along with their names.

The Maya also created a seasonal—or solar—calendar that told farmers when to plant their crops. This calendar had a year of 365 days, just like our calendar does. The Maya's year had 18 months with 20 days each, for a total of 360 days. Five days were added to the end of the year to make 365 days. This was done to make their year match the amount of time it took Earth to complete one orbit around the Sun.

The Mayan **pyramid** at Chichén Itzá (chee-CHEN eet-SAH) counts out the days of the solar calendar. Each of the pyramid's four sides has a stairway that leads to the temple at the top. Each of the stairways has 91 steps, for a total of 364 steps. The temple at the top sits on a platform, which adds 1 more step, for a total of 365 steps.

The pyramid at Chichén Itzá honored Kukulkan, the Mayan Wind God, who the Maya believed took the form of a snake with feathers. He connected Mayan rulers on Earth with the other Mayan gods. Kukulkan was also known as Quetzalcóatl.

The Aztec Calendar Stone

The **Aztecs** came to Mexico from the north in the 1100s. By the 1400s, they had become very powerful and started to conquer other people in the area. They adopted many practices from the people they conquered. From the Maya, the Aztecs adopted their sacred and solar calendars as well as their ideas about the history of the world.

The Aztecs and Maya believed that Earth's history had five ages, called Suns. At the end of each of the first four Suns, the world was destroyed, then re-created. The fifth Sun was the age the Aztec and Maya lived in. It is also the age we live in today.

The Aztecs carved a record of the world's history in a huge sculpture that is known as the Aztec calendar stone. At the center of the stone is the face of the Sun god, Tonatiuh (toh-nah-tee-OO-huh). Around Tonatiuh's face is a ring that holds four rectangles, which represent the first four Suns.

The Aztecs carved this enormous calendar stone in 1479. It is about 12 feet across and 3 feet thick. It weighs almost 25 tons, or 50,000 pounds!

The upper right rectangle represents the First Sun, when giants lived on Earth. It ended when jaguars ate the giants. The Second Sun, the upper left rectangle, was an age of farming. It ended when great winds blew everything away. Below that, the lower left rectangle represents the Third Sun, which was a time when great cities were built. Volcanoes destroyed that age. The lower right rectangle is the Fourth Sun, which was a time when the seas were filled with ships. A great flood ended that age.

The next ring of the calendar stone has the day signs that represent the 20 days of the sacred calendar. After that is the ring that represents the fifth, or present, age. The Aztecs believed this age would be destroyed by earthquakes. Finally, the outer ring shows two fire snakes, which represent the universe that surrounds Earth.

The calendar stone was originally part of a temple honoring the Sun god. At that time, it was painted with bright colors. The picture here gives us an idea of what it might have looked like then.

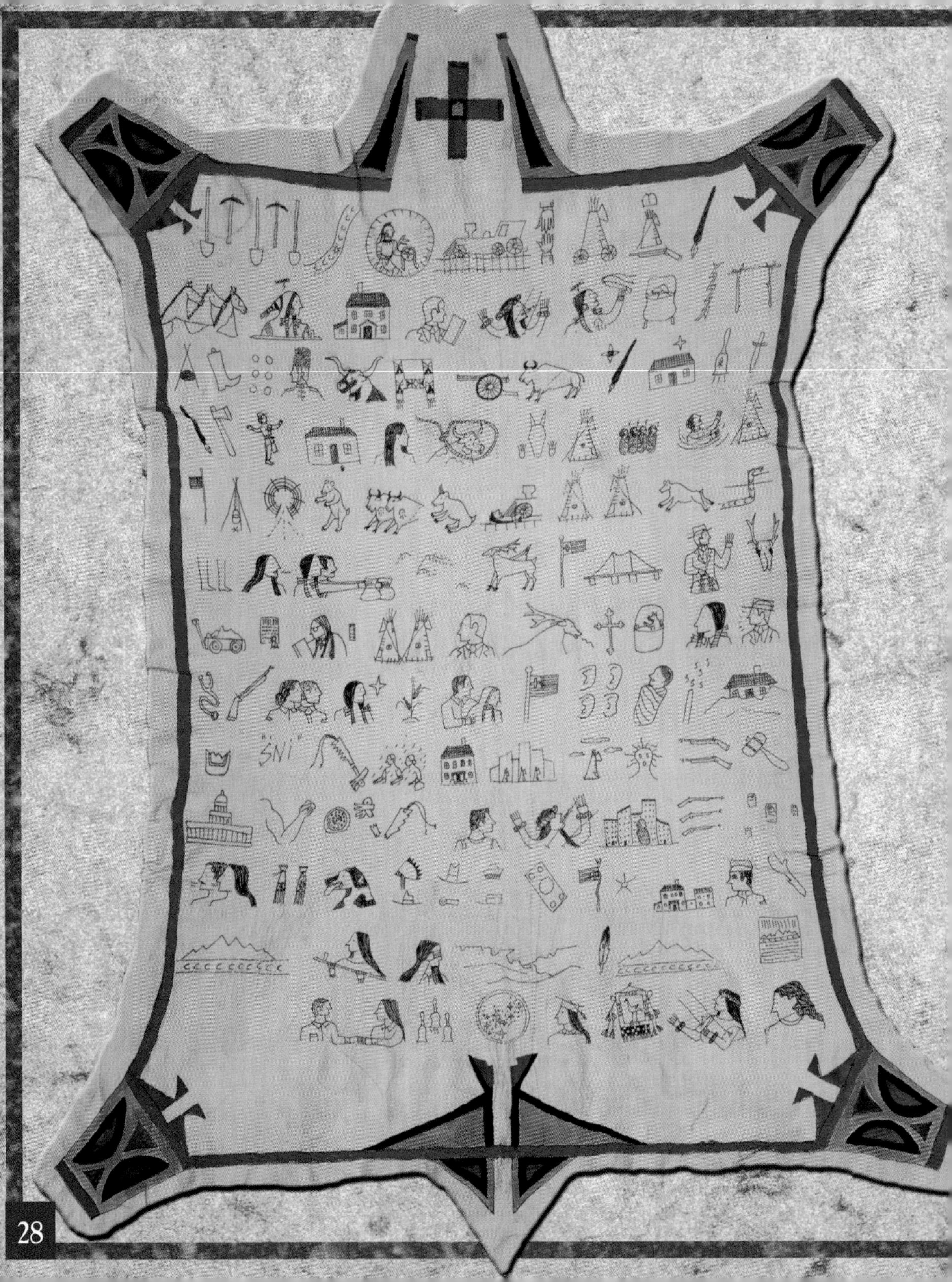
"ŚNI"

A Modern Native American Calendar

Today, many of the ancient ways of doing things have died out among Native Americans. However, some Native Americans are trying to bring back some of the old ways to remind others to take pride in their past. In 1995, a Sioux Indian named Dr. Thomas Red Owl Haukaas decided to make his own winter count. He was proud of the Sioux's history and wanted to make the kind of calendar that the Sioux had made in the past. He decided that his winter count would tell the history of the Sioux people in modern times.

Dr. Haukaas's winter count starts in 1868, when the U.S. government created the Rosebud **Reservation** in South Dakota for the Sioux people. It ends in 1993, 500 years after Christopher Columbus first encountered Native Americans in the "New World." That event had great meaning for Native Americans because it marked the beginning of enormous changes in their world.

Some pictographs from Dr. Haukaas's winter count are shown on page 30, along with their meanings.

Dr. Haukaas's winter count is arranged in rows. It starts in the upper right corner and goes to the left. Then the next row starts at the left and goes to the right. It continues going back and forth this way until the end.

Dr. Haukaas's Winter Count

1868–1869
A treaty created the Rosebud Reservation. Congress promised to protect the Sioux's lands.

1872–1873
Congress allowed the railroad to be built through Sioux hunting grounds.

1927–1928
Wildlife and plants died during a long drought.

1939–1940
Dr. Charles Eastman, the first Sioux medical doctor, died.

1978–1979
The Sioux set up their own radio station.

Dr. Haukaas's winter count tells about the suffering of the Sioux people, but it also tells about their many accomplishments. Dr. Haukaas wanted all Americans to be proud of the Sioux's history.

Glossary

astronomy (uh-STRAH-nuh-mee) The study of objects in space, such as the Sun, Moon, and stars.

axis (AK-suhs) An imaginary line that runs through the center of Earth from the North Pole to the South Pole.

Aztec (AZ-tek) A member of the group of Native Americans who ruled much of Mexico from 1428 to the 1520s.

ceremony (SAIR-uh-moh-nee) An event honoring the importance of something, often with music, dancing, and prayer.

Great Plains (GRAYT PLAYNZ) The area of flat or hilly land that covers most of the central United States and west-central Canada.

Maya (MY-uh) A group of Native Americans who created a great civilization in Mexico before they were conquered by the Aztecs in the 1400s.

new moon (NOO MOON) The time in the Moon's orbit around Earth when its dark side is facing Earth.

pictograph (PIK-tuh-graf) A picture or sign that is used in place of words in some writing systems.

pyramid (PEER-uh-mid) A building with a square base and four sloping sides that meet in a point or a small platform at the top.

reservation (re-zuhr-VAY-shun) An area of land set aside by the U.S. government for Native Americans to live on.

Sioux (SOO) A group of Native Americans who live on the Great Plains of North America and speak one of the Sioux languages.

spiral (SPY-ruhl) A curved shape that starts at a center point and winds out in larger and larger curls.

Index